Finger Paint and Pudding Prints

by Ann Sayre Wiseman

Addison-Wesley Publishing Company, Inc.
Reading, Massachusetts 01867
Printed in the United States of America
ABCDEFGHIJK-WZ-89876543210

ISBN 0-201-08346-9

 ADDISON-WESLEY

All You Need is

FINGER PAINT OR

 PUDDING

and 2 CLEAN HANDS

POUR
INSTANT
MIX INTO
BOWL

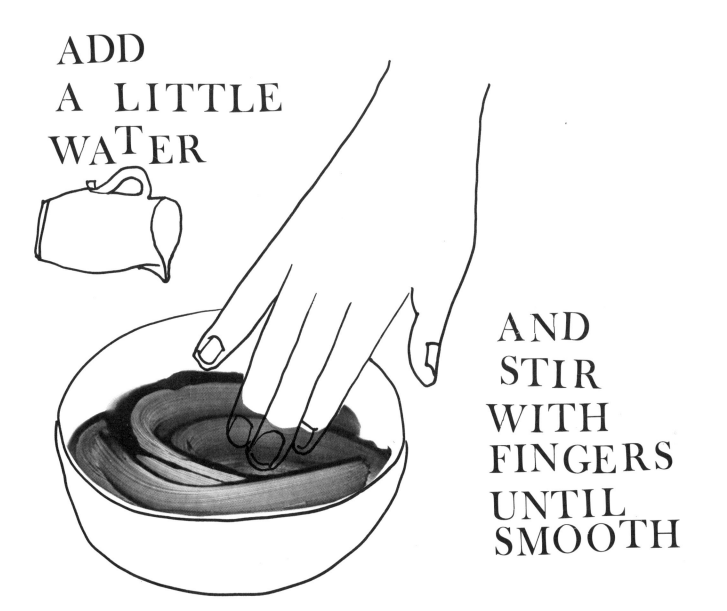

SCOOP
SOME
UP

SMEAR IT
ON A SHEET
OF PAPER
AND MESS
IT AROUND
NICE AND

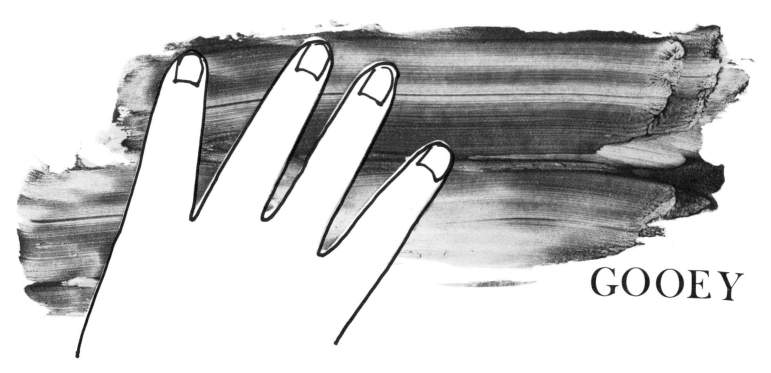

GOOEY

draw a serpent

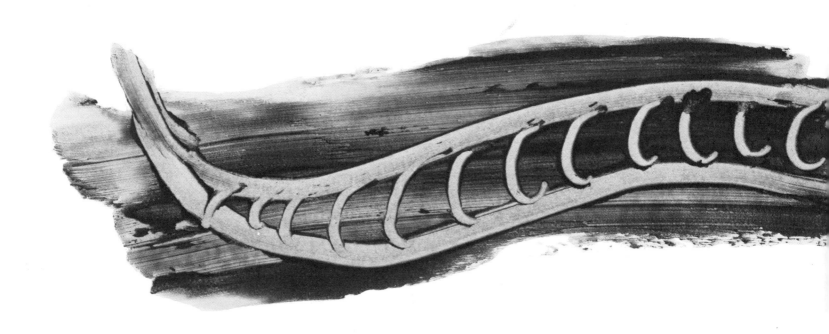

OR

zig zag zig zag zig zag with your fingers

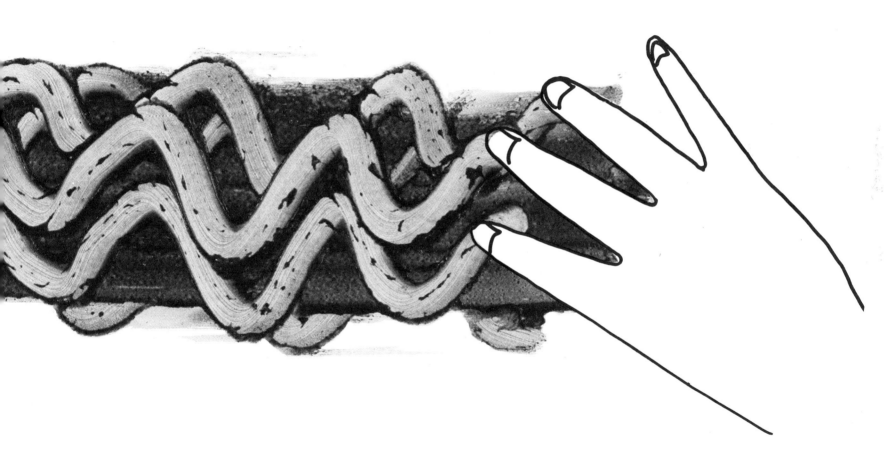

SMOOTH AWAY zig zags

and draw an angry SEA

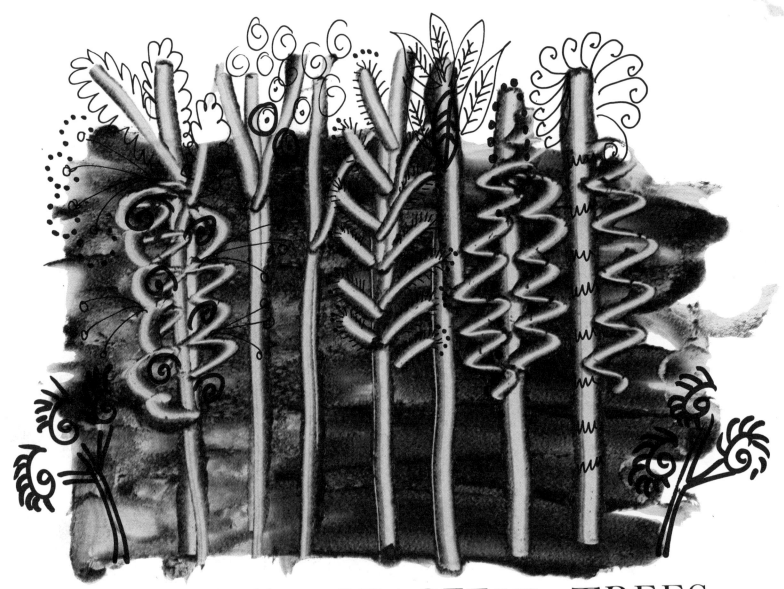

or a forest full of PEACEFUL TREES

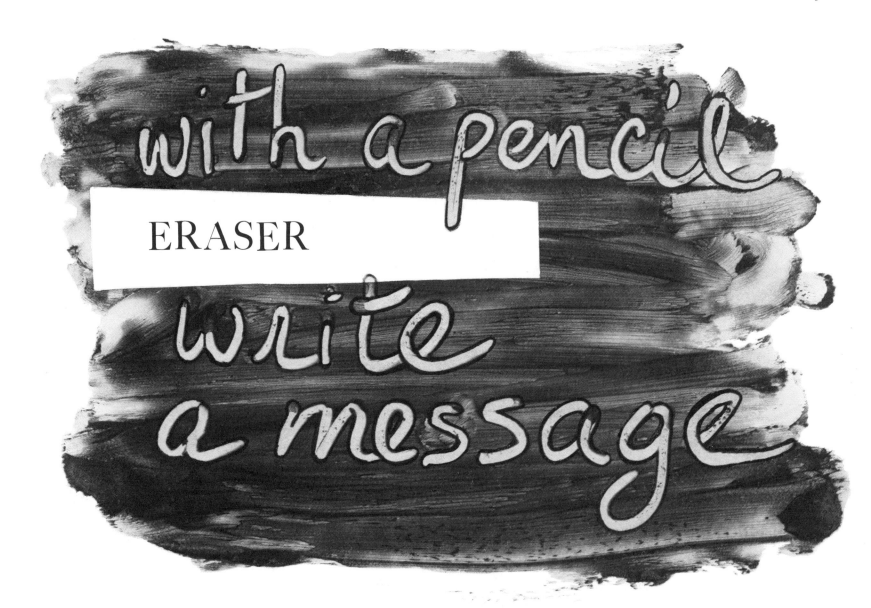

SCRIBBLE
AND
SCRATCH
WITH A
FORK

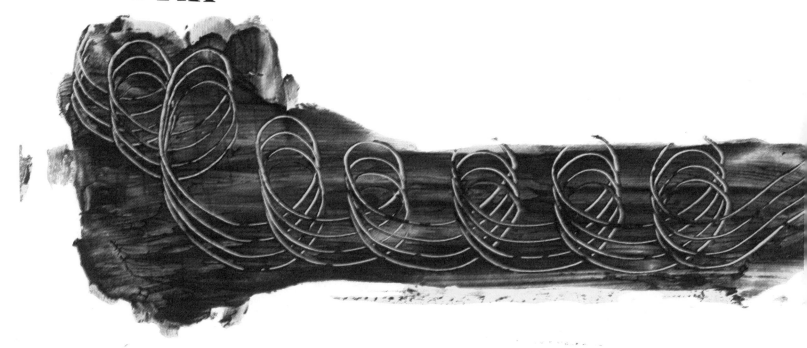

add
pen
line
details

you can

PRINT

your
pudding
picture

gently
lay a sheet
of thin paper
over your
picture
press
lightly and
lift up
slowly

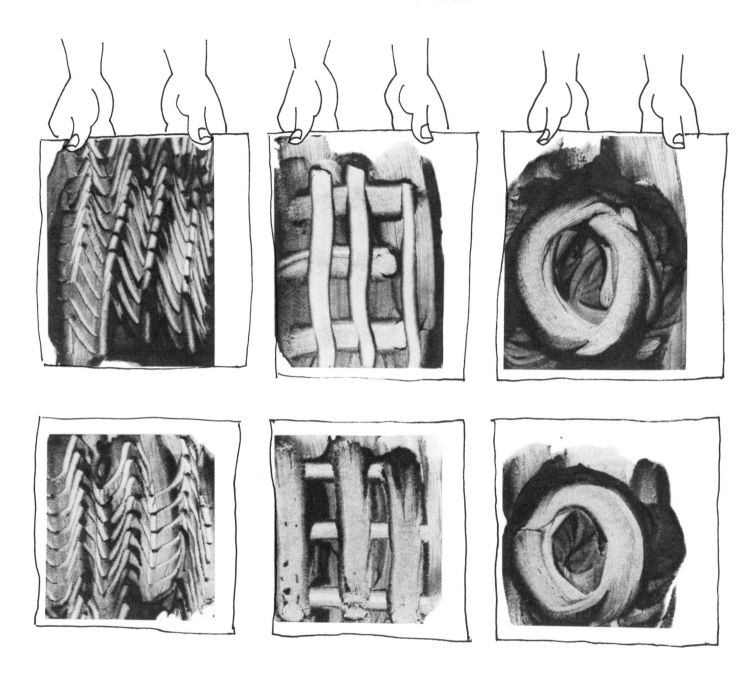

PRINT
A COLLECTION
OF
TEXTURES

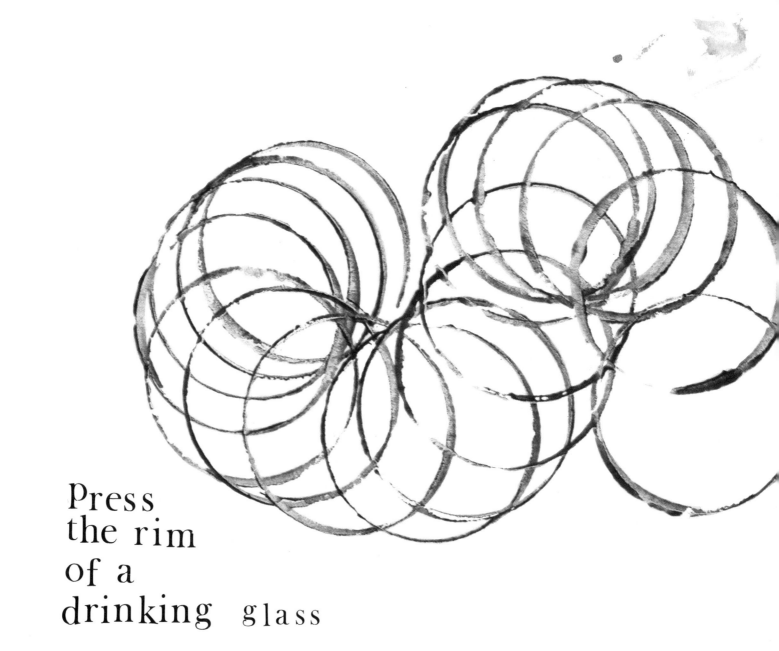

Press
the rim
of a
drinking glass

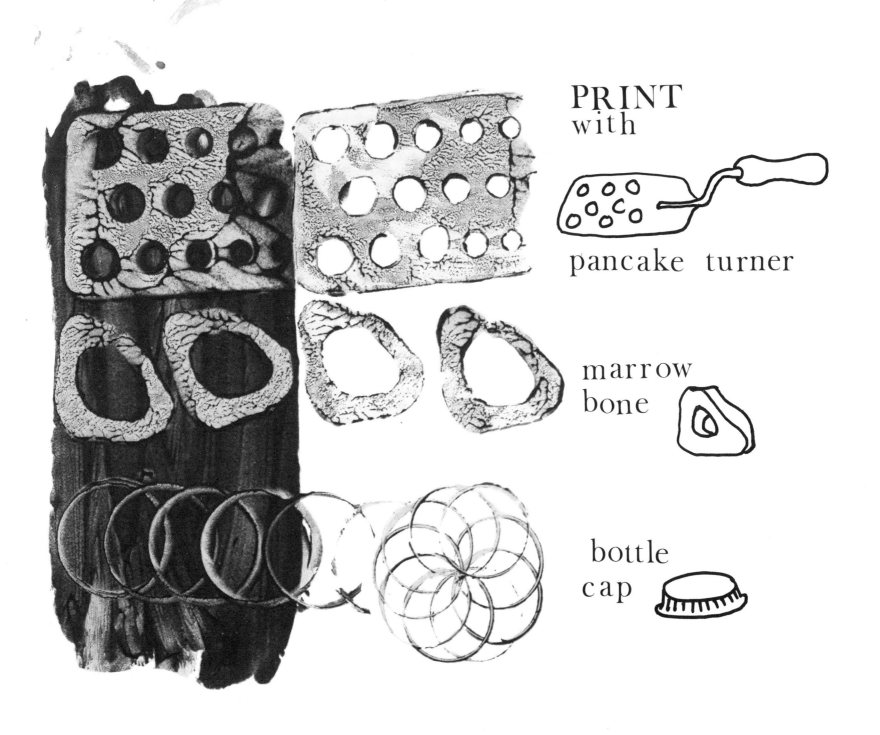

PRINT
with

pancake turner

marrow
bone

bottle
cap

PRINT
YOUR
FINGERS;
SEE WHAT
YOU CAN
MAKE
OUT
OF
THEM

IF YOU USE PUDDING

This Project

HAS A YUMMY ENDING

YOU MAY

Lick Your Fingers

if you use paint---wash them

Note to grownups

This book is designed to channel natural urges into self-expression.

It is permission to "mess about" in the process of creating art instead of wall prints and slapped hands.

The choice of instant chocolate pudding as a substitute for finger paint is not frivolous. It is cheap, non-toxic and always available.

Plan enough time and protected space so this adventure won't end in disaster. (Remember it is your attitude that either inhibits or frees creativity.)

Finger paint can be used directly on any hard, washable surface such as Formica, oil cloth or metal trays. You can use hard-surface paper like butcher paper, duplicating or typewriter paper — but find a way to hold it down to avoid suction problems —